dorset coast

front cover: catching first light at mudeford spit. back cover: broad bench, west of kimmeridge bay

it's a shore thing

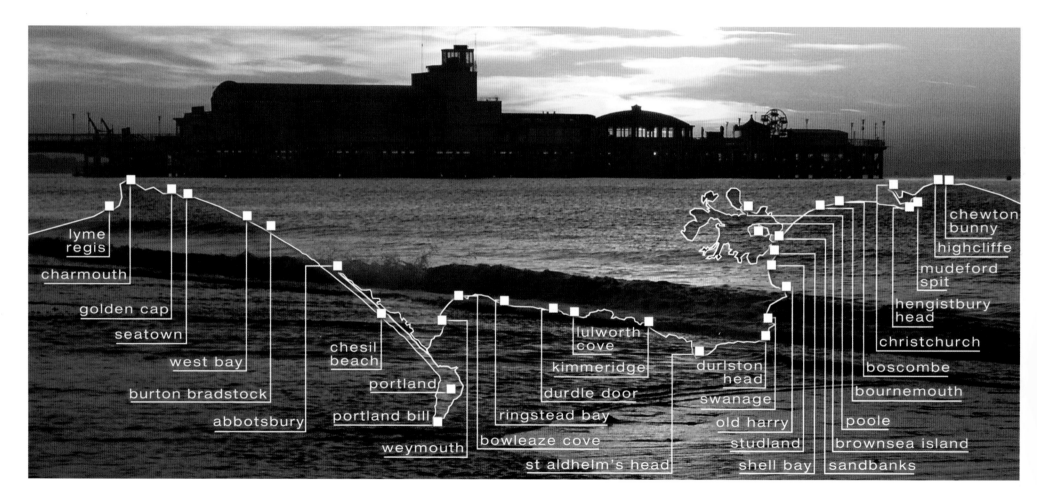

lyme
regis

charmouth

golden cap

seatown

west bay

burton bradstock

abbotsbury

chesil
beach

portland

portland bill

weymouth

bowleaze cove

st aldhelm's head

ringstead bay

lulworth
cove

kimmeridge

durdle door

durlston
head

swanage

old harry

studland

shell bay

chewton
bunny

highcliffe

mudeford
spit

hengistbury
head

christchurch

boscombe

bournemouth

poole

brownsea island

sandbanks

east to west

travel the coast from chewton bunny to lyme regis

foreword

by tom doyle, managing director of lloyds property group

"**P**EOPLE are drawn again and again to Dorset's coastline as if constantly seeing it through new eyes.

We are lucky to live in a county which meets the sea in a series of varied landscapes.

There are harbours, beaches, bays, cliffs, coves and marshes from Christchurch in the east to Lyme Regis in the west, providing some of England's most inspiring views over land and sea.

Specialising in the sale of coastal and waterside properties I know only too well how people favour living by the coast because of the light, the sea air,

the atmosphere, the lifestyle and the way it captures the imagination like nothing else can.

Even royalty has favoured this area over the years. King George III changed Weymouth's fortunes in the late 18th century after he was advised that bathing in the waters could cure his 'nervous disorder'. And the future King Edward VII bought a plot of land on Bournemouth's East Cliff where his mistress, Lillie Langtry, designed their love nest.

But plenty of this area's history is contained in the landscape itself, which shows evidence of the Earth's evolution dating back 185 million years.

As such, much of the Dorset coastline has been designated by UNESCO as England's first natural World Heritage Site, known as The Jurassic Coast.

Add into the mix resort towns, fossil cliffs, ports, pretty fishing villages, stone quays and marinas, and you have one of the most diverse stretches of coastline in the world, as the magnificent collection of photographs in this book will testify.

I am enormously proud to be associated with Dorset Coast – a fascinating pictorial tour along these world-famous shores.

Enjoy the journey!"

tom doyle

"the coast... it captures the imagination like nothing else can"

chewton bunny
to christchurch

tree-lined cliffs, quiet beaches
and ancient harbour settlement

in association with

LLOYDS
property group

chewton bunny to christchurch

a miraculous beam, replaced by jesus christ?

ACCORDING to local legend Christchurch gained its present name from the Norman Priory church built on the site of the original chapels which served the fortified Saxon burh of Twynham – the town between two rivers.

Medieval myths which sprang up around the building of the Priory suggested that it was originally planned to be on top of nearby St Catherine's Hill, but when the materials mysteriously moved to the harbourside location overnight, the architect decided this was a Divine signal.

The tale of the miraculous beam – which was cut too short only to be found the next day not only the right size but installed in the right place – coinciding with the disappearance of a carpenter who took neither food nor wages, (could it have been Jesus Christ himself?) added to the awe and aura of the Augustinian abbey. Its monks were widely famed for their medicine, especially the treatment of eye disorders cured with water drawn from their Pure Well.

The Priory became known as Christ's Church at Twynham and the name, corrupted and abbreviated to just Christchurch, was applied to the town.

Henry VIII stripped the Priory of its assets, demolished the monastic buildings and banished the monks in 1539 but allowed the townsfolk to keep their parish church – the longest in the country and larger than some cathedrals.

The nearby Norman castle was demolished in 1652 after Cromwell's Parliamentarians finally wrested the town from the Royalists during the Civil War.

did you know?

The Saxon Place Mill on the quayside was mentioned in the Domesday Book and was powered by the Mill Stream, a man-made tributary of the River Avon which flows into the harbour nearby.

Highcliffe Castle, containing elements of medieval masonry and stained glass from Normandy, was built in 1835 for retired diplomat Lord Stuart Rothesay, whose grandfather John Stuart, 3rd Earl of Bute, briefly British Prime Minister and ardent botanist, built the original High Cliff mansion there in 1773.

Stanpit Marsh is found just below the confluence of the Avon and Stour – the two rivers which gave the town its Saxon name of Tweoxneam.

The mix of salt and freshwater marshes provides vital habitat and feeding grounds for large numbers of wildlife species, especially migrating birds, and the site was declared a local nature reserve in 1964 and designated a Site of Special Scientific Interest in 1986.

Christchurch Priory is more than 900 years old and incorporates some of the Saxon chapels it replaced when Ranulf Flambard embarked on his ambitious building project in the reign of William II in 1094. The building was not completed until the late 15th century when the 120ft bell tower was built at the western end of the church to replace the original central spire which collapsed in 1420.

As well as its peal of 13 bells, two dating from the 14th century, the Priory rings to the sound of a massive 4,000-pipe organ, installed in 1999 at a cost of some £500,000 to replace the original 1788 instrument.

mudeford sandspit
holiday beach huts run from hengistbury head to mudeford quay

no hands on deck

...they must be swimming, at avon beach

'bunny' means chine or valley and this area has many that were used by smugglers to bring their contraband ashore

with sea to bow and stern, you can feel a million miles from the everyday. that's why mudeford beach huts have gone on sale for up to £160,000!

low light
the day fades away at hengistbury head

gone fishin'
waiting for a bite at christchurch harbour

walkers get their feet wet at highcliffe beach

stone survivor

described as our finest example of 'romantic picturesque', highcliffe castle has come through years of neglect, two severe fires, and demolition threats, to be restored in the 1990s

miracle beam

legend has it that a beam, cut too short during the priory's construction, had regained its length and appeared in position the next morning. it is there today an idyllic place to let a little time float by

hot hut

this hut was on the market for £130,000!

quay to the harbour
mudeford quay, mudeford spit and hengistbury head beyond

holy waters
the stour and avon rivers meet below the priory, before flowing into christchurch harbour

bournemouth

from barren heathland, to retreat
for the wealthy, to holiday resort

in association with

LLOYDS
property group

bournemouth

a buzzing vibrant beach resort nearing its bicentenary

FAMOUSLY blessed with seven miles of golden sands, Bournemouth is a thoroughly modern English resort town boasting shops and restaurants to rival any major city, a buzzing nightlife, watersports and award-winning gardens, yet well within reach of the peace and quiet of open countryside.

A relatively young town – it is due to celebrate its bicentenary in 2010 – Bournemouth grew from a series of small villages and hamlets, including familiar names such as Holdenhurst, Throop and Kinson where the locals eked out a living from the surrounding heathland.

During the 18th century, most of the action around Bournemouth centred on smuggling – indeed, one of the country's most successful outlaws, Isaac Gulliver, led a gang called the White Wigs until his pardon in 1782 when he settled down in Kinson to enjoy the fruits of his endeavours.

Bournemouth and its near neighbour, the spa town of Boscombe, started to grow from the turn of the 19th century as the wealthy and infirm sought the restorative benefits of the sea air.

Generally acknowledged as the founder of Bournemouth, Captain Lewis Tregonwell of the Dorset

Yeomanry built the town's first private house – now part of the Royal Exeter Hotel – in 1810 and the town began to expand outwards from the seafront.

The first pier opened in 1856. In 1880 a new metal structure was formally opened and lasted, with many alterations, until the Second World War when it was demolished so as to hinder any invasion. The current pier was built soon after the war, with the Pier Theatre being added in 1957.

did you know?

■ Like most of the small inlets and chines, Branksome Chine is said to have been a regular route for 18th century smugglers as they headed inland to their hideaways in the Kinson area. It also has a link with John Betjeman, the famous Poet Laureate, who once wrote: "Walk the asphalt path of Branksome Chine / In resin-scented air like strong Greek wine."

■ In 1892, the 18-year-old Winston Churchill fell 30 feet to the ground from a bridge over one of the chines. He lay unconscious for three days and was bed-ridden for three months.

■ Robert Louis Stevenson came to Westbourne in 1884, suffering from TB. Now marked by a garden at the end of Robert Louis Stevenson Avenue, his house, Skerryvore, was named after a lighthouse built by his family's company. He wrote Dr Jekyll and Mr Hyde while living there.

■ The Dorset Belles have been ferrying pleasure cruisers from Bournemouth Pier since 1868 when the steamer Fawn was chartered for a trip to Spithead, where a review of the fleet was being held in honour of the Shah of Persia. Boat trips still run today, with the paddle steamer Waverley and her motorised companion Balmoral.

■ Captain Charles Rolls – of Rolls-Royce car company fame – became Britain's first aviation fatality when his biplane broke up in mid-air at Bournemouth International Aviation Meeting on July 12, 1910.

■ The future King Edward VII built The Red House, on Bournemouth's East Cliff, in 1877 as a romantic love nest he could share with his actress mistress Lillie Langtry. Among many interesting features is a peep hole through which His Royal Highness could spy on his guests before deciding whether to join them. The house is now run as the Langtry Manor Hotel.

pier support
having undergone many transformations, bournemouth pier still stands at the heart of a thriving tourist industry

21

it's important not to overdo it when sunbathing: reapplying sun block creams, and getting into shade in the middle of the day is a good idea

it's a tough job...

up to 100,000 people catch some rays on the beaches on a summer weekend

waterworld
thousands of people enjoy time afloat in the bay

after some years of neglect, boscombe pier has undergone much-needed renovation

pier pressure
for too long boscombe pier has been the poor relation

pier pleasure
bournemouth pier, just below bournemouth's central gardens, on seven miles of golden sands

it's a gas: all kinds of balloons
at pier approach

walk on water
treading the boards at the pier theatre

balloon with a view
the bournemouth eye gives breathtaking views... if you have a head for heights

just add water

construction works

blue flag fun

safe beaches are paradise for children, making memories that will stay with them

surf silhouettes

hot seats

100,000 is a crowd

summer bank holiday weekends see peak numbers hit the sand

rooms with a view

little huts all in a row

paddle team
row, row, row your boat

groynes stop the sand from being washed away by longshore drift

coast

need a lift? at east cliff

making waves: 'the waterfront' building, has proved to be a controversial issue with residents and visitors alike

highs and lows
some waterfront properties are larger than others

pier point
today's bournemouth pier. the town's first wooden jetty was constructed in 1856

hot in the shade

catching some colour behind a windbreak

poole

ancient port, blue flag beaches
and 'millionaires' row'

a massive natural harbour, second in size only to sydney

HOME to the world's second largest natural harbour, complete with its own network of islands, beautiful beaches, marshes and heathland, Mother Nature was clearly enjoying herself when she fashioned the coastline around Poole.

It supports a wealth of human activity – both at work and play – as well as a huge variety of flora and fauna.

The busy harbour is home to all manner of commercial shipping, from container shipping to the cross-Channel ferries, as well as a thriving fishing industry and the ancilliary enterprises.

The internationally-known Sunseeker superboats are built here for well-heeled customers from James Bond to Roman Abramovich.

The harbour is also hugely popular with the watersports community, dedicated sailors and pleasure boaters, making it some of the busiest – and most difficult to manage – water in the country.

But the earliest evidence of human activity dates from 295BC, the date ascribed to a logboat excavated off Brownsea Island in 1964.

To the south and west of the Harbour are important wildlife habitats, including the five islands, the biggest and best known of which, Brownsea, is a haven for red squirrels, peacocks and deer. Conservationists have also celebrated some important successes in Poole Harbour, particularly in boosting numbers of the once-rare little egret.

On the southern shore is Europe's largest onshore oil field, Wytch Farm. Hidden by a forest of conifers, the drilling extracts oil from a vast submarine field and currently produces more than 3.4 million tonnes per year.

did you know?

▓ Harry Paye, the original Poole pirate, so incensed the French and Spanish with his constant raiding of their coastal towns, they sent a combined force to attack the unfortified Poole in 1405. Having been driven back to Canford Heath the locals rallied and turned on their attackers, forcing them back to their ships.

▓ Sandbanks Beach has both the EU Blue Flag and the Tidy Britain Group's Seaside Award, its three miles of fine, golden sand gradually sloping down to clean, safe water.

▓ BOAC – the forerunner of BA – ran its first transatlantic flying boat passenger service from Poole Harbour on August 3, 1940.

▓ Poole is home to the HQ of the Royal National Lifeboat Institution and trains lifeboat crews from all over the world. It also has the country's busiest lifeboat station.

▓ Although there is no record of Poole in the Domesday Book of 1086, it was part of the manor of Canford. The main port for the area at that time was Wareham, but as the Frome silted up, traders moved to take advantage of the deeper waters, establishing the town of Poole in the late 12th century.

▓ The world-famous Poole Pottery was established in 1873 as Carter's Industrial Tile Manufactory on the quayside where production continued until 1999 when it was switched to a new factory.

▓ With property prices outstripping those in Manhattan, Mayfair and Tokyo, so-called Millionaires' Row on Sandbanks is one of the world's most expensive places to live. The area has caught the attention of celebrities including Liam Gallagher, Kylie Minogue and the Beckhams – although none has actually bought a home there.

one of the many long-established hostelries along poole quay

action

poole has a busy commercial port with ferries, cargo ships and fishing vessels operating in and around the leisure boats

moor parking
there are several marinas for the large local sailing community

■ left, royal motor yacht club, sandbanks

■ above, parkstone yacht club

■ below, salterns point marina

dolphin quays under construction, on the old poole pottery site

little and large

all sizes of craft inhabit poole harbour

winter sails
hardy souls hit the waves all year round

coast

rising road
the bridge at poole quay lifts to allow tall and masted vessels to pass through

waterworks

shoppers, traders, pub-goers, yachtsmen, fishermen and tourists rub shoulders at poole quay

quay hole
waters from holes bay pour in and out past poole quay with each tide

brownsea

the island, now owned by the national trust, provided the inspiration for enid blyton's 'keep-away island'

coast

- below: brownsea island
- small image: furzey island
- far right: a pleasure boat arrives at brownsea

island life

there are many islands in poole harbour. brownsea is sanctuary for one of our last red squirrel colonies

island castle

brownsea's branksea castle viewed across poole harbour from sandbanks

hotting up
the new day arrives over sandbanks

sundown
a brittany ferries vessel negotiates the channel in poole harbour at the start of a night crossing to france

cold harbour

winter storm flooding at shore road, sandbanks

POOLE BEACHES

SANDBANKS

CAUTION

w a r m   f r o n t

the heat is on: a summer's day on sandbanks beach

■ sailing by 'millionaires' row'

■ "on reflection, maybe there's not enough wind"

early birds

low tide bait digging attracts some aerial attention

front lines
a flat day at sandbanks

chain link

sandbanks ferry is the gateway to, and from, studland and the isle of purbeck

■ crossing point: the first sailing of a vehicle-carrying ferry between sandbanks and south haven point was on july 15, 1926. coal-fired and steam-driven, it was popular straight away and in its first, short, summer season it carried 12,000 cars and 100,000 passengers! the fare, one way, was 2s 6d (12.5p) per car and 3d (less than 1.5p) per passenger. today's ferry, the bramble bush bay, entered service in january 1994 and carries up to 48 cars

shell bay to ballard down

the 'jurassic coast' starts here

in association with

LLOYDS
property group

coast
shell bay to ballard down

sand dunes, sheer white cliffs and tales of king arthur

TO cross the chain link ferry from Sandbanks to Studland is to take a welcome step back in time, from the cosmopolitan bustle of Millionaires' Row to the open space of unspoilt heathland and beach.

Best known for its beautiful sand and safe bathing, Shell Bay is one of Dorset's finest natural attractions. Ecologically stable and largely self-sustaining, the wind-blown sand dunes protect the beach and provide a habitat for a rich diversity of wildlife and plants.

The dunes also protect a small lagoon known as Little Sea into which Sir Belvedere is supposed to have cast King Arthur's Excalibur. It's a great tale, but research dates the formation of Little Sea to the 17th century at the earliest.

The grand sweep of Studland Bay gives way to the distinctive stack of Old Harry Rocks, which forms the eastern end of the Jurassic Coast World Heritage Site and is all that remains of a ridge that once bordered Poole Bay when it was dry land. Much of the area's pre-history lies buried beneath the harbour mud, but it once provided good hunting grounds for the first human inhabitants.

Rounding the point by sea provides a fine view of Ballard Down, the chalk down that forms a headland between Studland and the resort town of Swanage. Its grasslands remained untouched for thousands of years until demand for agricultural land saw much of it turned over to arable farming in the Second World War. Today, the National Trust owns the Down and has overseen its return to nature.

did you know?

Studland Beach was the setting of the opening scene from the first episode of Monty Python's Flying Circus in which Michael Palin staggered out of the sea, collapsed on the sand and proclaimed: "It's…" The promo video for Coldplay's breakthrough hit Yellow was also filmed there.

Legend has it that the Devil went to sleep on Old Harry Rocks, which led to the old euphemism of the Devil being called Old Harry. The Devil must have been busy around Studland, as local lore also explains the 400-ton Agglestone Rock, which stands on a mound on the heath, was thrown there from the Isle of Wight by an enraged Lucifer.

Studland Heath is one of only a few places in Britain which is home to all six native reptile species – adder, grass snake, smooth snake, slow worm, common lizard and sand lizard.

In April 1944, King George VI, General Montgomery and General Eisenhower watched Allied troops taking part in Exercise Tiger, training for the Normandy landings, on Studland beach. Their observation point, Fort Henry, is owned by the National Trust and can be visited at Redend Point.

The Studland peninsula also supports Britain's most popular naturist beach and British Naturism works with the owners, the National Trust, to keep Studland family friendly. The area has been used by naturists since the late 19th century.

The Bloomsbury Set, a loose collective of free-spirited bohemians including Virginia Woolf, EM Forster, Vanessa Bell, Lytton Strachey and the economist John Maynard Keynes, adopted Studland as a holiday home from around 1910 until the outbreak of the First World War.

old harry and the pinnacles
sculpted by centuries of erosion by the sea

coast

flora among the dunes at studland

beware: you may see a full moon, in the middle of the day!

fortification of the beach

NATURISTS MAY BE SEEN BEYOND THIS POINT

"it's..." studland bay

these sands saw the emergence of palin and python

breezing it
wind powers much of the entertainment

shelter
watercraft moored below the headland

coast

from ballard down you look onto swanage and the bay

water colour

kayaks on the sand at knoll beach

a float
moored in the lee of old harry

HEATHER WALK
SAND DUNE TRAIL

dune roaming
behind the beach, coarse grasses and heathers bind the sand

sail to the isle
taking the ferry to studland saves a 25-30 mile drive around the harbour

swanage to man o'war

classic family resort and a coast shaped by prehistoric forces

in association with

LLOYDS property group

coast
swanage to man o'war

walk along the edge of prehistory

THE beauty of Dorset's coastline is limitless, but the stretch from Swanage to Durdle Door is almost sublime.

Today's Swanage oozes the genteel calm of a classic English resort, but less than a hundred years ago it was a busy port for the shipping of Purbeck stone hewn from the countless quarries that once peppered the hills above the town.

On Purbeck's south-eastern tip, just a mile outside Swanage, is the 280-acre Durlston Country Park, a veritable paradise for nature lovers. It encompasses sea cliffs, coastal limestone downland, hay meadows, hedgerows and woodland; and provides a home for 34 species of butterfly as well as a vantage point for dolphin-watching.

One of Purbeck's lost treasures, Tilly Whim Caves, is now closed to the public. The Coast Path takes you past the caves on the way to the fossil-strewn Dancing Ledge and the rough charm of St Aldhelm's Head.

One of many small coves carved from the coast, Chapman's Pool offers plenty of scope for fossil hunters; as does nearby Kimmeridge, overlooked by the famous Clavell Tower.

The atmospheric ghost village of Tyneham nestles in the valley leading to Worbarrow Bay and has stood empty since it was evacuated a few days before Christmas 1943 to allow British and American troops to train. The villagers were never allowed back to their homes, which have all but returned to nature along with the nearby Tyneham House, which remains off limits.

The Jurassic Coast boasts several fossil forests and ancient sea shores. None is better preserved than the one at East Lulworth which whets the appetite for the impressive Lulworth Cove, one of Dorset's most recognisable landmarks.

did you know?

At St Aldhelm's Head is the site of the 12th century Chapel of St Aldhelm and a stainless steel sculpture commemorating the radar research carried out at RAF Worth Matravers during World War Two.

One of the "nodding donkey" beam pumps at Kimmeridge has been pumping continuously since production began in 1959, and is the oldest continuously pumping oil well in the world.

Clavell Tower at Kimmeridge has been dismantled and is being rebuilt 25 metres back from the crumbling cliff edge.

Sadly out of bounds during the week, but open most weekends, the beach at Mupe Bay below Bindon Hill is one of the few shingle beaches on this stretch of coast. The beach at nearby Arish Mel, meanwhile, was a popular landing place for smugglers in the 18th century.

Soldier-poet Rupert Brooke wrote some of his finest work while stationed at Lulworth Camp. He also spent time on holiday at Lulworth Cove, suffering a breakdown there just after Christmas 1911 while staying with members of the free-spirited Bloomsbury set.

The poet John Keats famously left England forever from Lulworth and headed to Rome in 1820 having written the poem Bright Star, Would I Were Steadfast in Lulworth the year before. In 1920, Thomas Hardy wrote At Lulworth Cove, A Century Back about Keats' departure.

Dancing Ledge, near Langton Matravers, was so called because the stone cut out of it – used to build Ramsgate Harbour in Kent – was the same size as a ballroom dancefloor!

Many locals feel Stair Hole is the more impressive of Dorset's blow hole coves – there are two arches there and a staggering example of the contorted limestone rocks known as the Lulworth Crumple.

crumple zone
a history of violence shown in the contorted rock strata above stair hole

coast

■ 'greek columns' in prince albert gardens that used to adorn a london building. they are the same as those on the front of the british museum, part of a collection of items shipped in from london sites

little london by the sea

swanage pier has undergone a full restoration in recent years

nestling in an east-facing bay that sweeps round from ballard point to peveril point, sheltered from the prevailing winds

■ the globe was installed in 1887
a year after durlston castle,
above it, was built

circumnavigation
around the world at durlston

wonder world
the great globe in durlston country park, made from portland limestone, weighs a massive 40 tons

tilly whim

the caves, between durlston head and anvil point, were limestone quarries mainly worked during the 18th century. they are now unsafe and closed to the public

anvil point lighthouse is a waypoint for vessels in the channel. built of local stone, it was opened in 1881 by neville chamberlain's father, as transport minister

chapman's pool

a variety of flora thrives along the dorset coast

shear drops

looking down on chapman's pool, purbeck sheep often graze fields that run along the cliff top

nearer thy god

probably dating from the early 12th century st aldhelm's chapel, named after the bishop of sherborne who died in 709, sits atop the head near to the coastwatch station

coast

eldon seat

lines of rock strata run underwater out into the bay

tower
clavell tower, a folly built in 1831, had become increasingly endangered by the receding cliff, so it is being moved back 25 metres and restored

kimmeridge
swell rushes over the rock ledges

take a seat
low tide at broad bench

coast

gad cliff & worbarrow tout

mass movement

gad cliff

88

room for one

worbarrow tout watches over a yacht that has squeezed into worbarrow bay

haven

lulworth cove provides safe waters for paddlers and fishing boats alike... and others

studied in schools up and down the country, lulworth cove is a perfect illustration of the erosive power of the sea

holiday haven
sunny lulworth cove

s t a i r   h o l e
one of the dorset coast's famous rock arches

red sky at night

west lulworth delight

deep stare

gazing down into stair hole

coast

st oswald's and man o'war bays

'man o'war' rocks 'afloat' just offshore

durdle door to bowleaze cove

rock arches, sheer cliffs
and quiet coves

in association with

LLOYDS
property group

durdle door to bowleaze cove

secluded bays and sea stacks

THE coastline between Lulworth Cove and Bowleaze Cove near Weymouth is one of the most rugged and beautiful yet peaceful parts of Dorset's seascape.

The hills and cliffs rise and fall with the dramatic contours of the land; the South West Coast Path perched precariously on the edge and the pounding sea far below. With little or no habitation, the area is left to the wind, wildlife and walkers.

It is ideal for walking, with great swathes of greensward and agriculture on one side and views across the channel on the other. It's no wonder many people describe this stretch of coastline as their favourite place.

The most recognisable landmark on the Jurassic Coast, perhaps even the whole south coast, is Durdle Door.

This magnificent 65ft arch was formed by the sea eroding softer rocks and leaving behind the hard limestone. It seems to take on different hues depending on the angle of the sun.

Access to the great arch is either by a half-mile walk from Lulworth Cove or a drive through the adjacent holiday park to a parking site.

To the west are the impressive cliff of Bat's Head, the four sea stacks known as the Calf, the Cow, the Blind Cow and the Bull and the imposing Swyre Head.

The massive cliff at White Nothe (also referred to as White Nose), east of Ringstead, is a mixture of crumbling chalk and thin grass cover. A huge landslide is a dominant feature. The hills above Ringstead offer superb views of Portland and the coastline.

The small River Jordan reaches the sea at Bowleaze Cove, on the outskirts of Weymouth. From there to Weymouth centre is a long stretch of beach, gradually turning from shingle to sand.

did you know?

▓ A landslip in 1826 near the White Nothe cliffs created the phenomenon known as Burning Cliff, when a chemical reaction caused the organic-rich clays to start smouldering. It had the appearance of a volcanic eruption and anyone getting too close to the smoke felt dizzy.

▓ The deserted medieval village of Ringstead was decimated by, according to who you believe, economic troubles, Black Death or pillaging French pirates. It became a centre for smuggling, and is now an area good for fossils, particularly in the Kimmeridge Clay cliffs.

▓ The Smugglers Inn at Osmington Mills has one of the best pub car parks in Britain – just for the views across to Portland. The building is said to date from the 13th century and was once home to Emmanuel Charles, leader of an infamous gang of smugglers.

▓ The striking Art Deco Riviera Hotel overlooking the sea at Bowleaze Cove was built in 1937. The white structure is a listed building and visible for miles.

▓ The painter John Constable spent much time, including his honeymoon, in Osmington due to his friendship with the village rector, Archdeacon John Fisher. He painted many local landscapes including one of Bowleaze, now hanging in the National Gallery.

▓ On the hill behind Bowleaze Cove lies the Jordan Hill Roman Temple, or rather, the square foundations of a 4th century Romano-Celtic temple.

▓ Many stories have grown up around the origins of the white horse chalk figure on Osmington Hill. Depicting George III, the king never saw it as it was carved after his last visit to Weymouth. Did the creator really commit suicide when he realised his subject was facing the wrong way – out of town?

standing firm: the limestone outcrop that produced the durdle door rock arch

man o'war

looking west, man o'war, durdle door, swyre head, bat's head and white nothe

over arching
bird's eye view of the world famous arch

night light
glowing outside 'the door'

▨ under attack: bat's head already has an arch formation, which may develop over many, many years into a stack like old harry and the needles

▨ landslips at swyre head

lights out
sun dipping down behind portland

coast

sea cows
the view across ringstead bay to weymouth

brooding
the door's character changes with the light

atop white nothe

h i g h   p o i n t . . .

some make more effort than others to get that special view

idyllic
dropping anchor in ringstead bay

fresh water cascades towards
salt at osmington mills

big bill

the view towards portland from above ringstead bay

hard water
rocks in the surf at osmington

art house: built in 1937 the listed art deco riviera hotel above bowleaze cove is visible for miles around

bowleaze
at the north-eastern edge of weymouth

weymouth

a fashionable resort,
thanks to a king's patronage

in association with

LLOYDS
property group

weymouth

a sweeping georgian seafront at 'england's bay of naples'

WEYMOUTH is very much the traditional seaside resort. Its crowning glory is the golden sand of the impressive beach backed by the elegant sweep of the Georgian seafront.

Thousands of holidaymakers pour in each summer to enjoy the bucket and spade lifestyle as well as the many attractions in close proximity, such as wildlife centres, country parks and nature reserves.

Easy access to Dorset's dramatic World Heritage status Jurassic Coast has also made Weymouth the destination for growing numbers of tourists seeking more active breaks.

The bustling harbour is at the very heart of the town with ferries, fishing boats and charter vessels all vying for space.

The resort's marina is usually packed with yachts and the nearby Nothe Fort offers commanding views of the coastline and town. Restaurants and pubs hug the harbourside.

Weymouth is named after the River Wey and records of habitation stretch back to 934AD. Originally two towns on either side of the harbour, Weymouth and Melcombe Regis both grew prosperous as ports, before they were united in 1571.

The town was ransacked by the French, fought over in the Civil War and played a major role in the D-Day landings of 1944.

The Black Death came to England via the port, the world's first bathing machines were established in the town and King George III popularised the seaside holiday in Weymouth.

Today's visitors enjoy a host of festivals, ranging from military commemorations to beach volleyball, and one of Britain's biggest New Year's Eve celebrations is hosted by Weymouth.

did you know?

■ Weymouth's links with the America's Cup stretch back to 1903 when Sir Thomas Lipton's Shamrock III was dismasted during a sudden squall while undergoing trials in Weymouth Bay on April 17. One crew member was drowned.

■ The Black Death, or bubonic plague, arrived in England in 1348 through Melcombe Regis, then a separate town to neighbouring Weymouth, carried by a sailor from Gascony. By the end of the year it had spread throughout the West Country, killing up to 50 per cent of the population and causing the beginning of the end of the feudal system.

■ The Cutty Sark, the world's only surviving tea clipper, was given to the nation by Weymouth widow Catherine Dowman in 1948. Her husband, Capt Wilfred Dowman, had rescued the vessel from a Portuguese shipyard in 1922 and lovingly restored her. The ship was damaged by fire in dry dock at Greenwich in 2007.

■ Sand sculptor Fred Darrington spent nearly 50 years making elaborate models on Weymouth beach – ranging from King Kong to the Last Supper – using only sand and water, until his retirement in 1996. His grandson Mark Anderson continues the tradition today.

■ US troops left Weymouth in June 1944 for the bloody D-Day battles on Omaha Beach, Normandy. In total, half-a-million military personnel passed through the town in the following months.

■ The 44ft landmark Jubilee Clock on Weymouth Esplanade commemorates the 1887 Golden Jubilee of Queen Victoria. It was unveiled in 1888, but not brightly painted until the 1920s. It stood on a platform on the beach until the esplanade was widened.

■ The statue of George III on Weymouth seafront celebrates the 50th year of his reign and was unveiled in October 1810.

decked out
nothing to do, and all day to do it

rain or shine

we do like to be beside the seaside

reflected glory
weymouth's classic georgian esplanade

air port
various 'aircraft' around the town, some more successful than others

sands of time
weymouth retains its popularity with beachgoers, here on carnival day

coast

sea horse: enjoying a winter's day paddle

water ride

in the saddle on the beach

coast

cross channel ferries operate
side by side with fishing boats

water works

as well as a resort, weymouth is very much a working port

yacht spot
2012's olympic sailing events will be staged at weymouth

there have been a number of town bridges, the first dating back to the late 16th century

if the bridge is up you can cross the harbour by ferry

FERRY ACROSS THE HARBOUR TO

NOTHE FORT & GARDENS
BREWERS QUAY
AND
CAR PARKS
FARE 50 P.
EACH
Q AT TOP OF STEPS

pivotal role

weymouth town bridge was opened in 1930 by the then duke of york, later to be george vi

at sandsfoot castle ruins

colours at greenhill gardens

t r a n q u i l l i t y   b a s e
enjoying the space at nothe gardens

nothe fort: constructed between 1860 and 1872, by royal engineers and inmates from portland prison, it was part of a series of south coast fortifications against perceived french aggression

ancient & modern

nothe fort watches over the harbour entrance, nearby the pavilion site will be redeveloped as part of the 2012 olympics preparations

portland

'carved by time out of a single stone'
- thomas hardy

in association with

LLOYDS
property group

portland

for centuries the isle has exported stone around the world

PORTLAND is an explorer's island with curiosities of history and folklore just waiting to be discovered

It is a striking tilted table of limestone four-and-a-half miles long and one-and-three-quarter miles wide, rising to nearly 500ft before sloping gently south towards Portland Bill and the famous 135ft lighthouse, and two earlier lighthouses nearby.

Joined to the mainland by Chesil Beach and a public road bridge, the Isle has scenery and an isolated quality that contrasts dramatically with neighbouring Weymouth. It has few trees, extensive quarries and a stark beauty, and is now central to the Dorset coastline's World Heritage Site status.

The Isle and Royal Manor of Portland, known to Thomas Hardy as the Isle of Slingers, has three castles, three lighthouses, wildlife in abundance, tiny coves, sheer cliffs and excellent sporting facilities.

The former naval base has changed ownership. Now known as Portland Port, it is fast becoming a booming industrial and maritime area.

These waters are a haven for fishermen and divers. Onshore and off, plants and animals provide a wealth of interest for visitors to Chesil Beach and Portland.

The area's unique geology and its position have ensured that many parts of the Island, including the whole of the coastline, are designated as Sites of Special Scientific Interest, and Chesil Beach and the Fleet lagoon are conservation sites of international importance.

Portland is a haven for watersports. It is considered to be the top spot for sea angling in Britain and there are hundreds of wrecks, from fine liners to submarines, to hold a diver spellbound.

did you know?

The only two surviving Mulberry Harbours, built to provide temporary harbours for the 1944 D-Day landings, stand in Portland Harbour. Each of these giant concrete structures is more than 200 feet long and weighs nearly 8,000 tons. Others were sent to the Netherlands in the 1950s to be used as sea defences.

The thatched Avice's Cottage at Wakeham, Portland, dates from 1640 and houses Portland Museum, but was once home to contraception pioneer Dr Marie Stopes. She gave the cottage to the island and was the museum's first curator.

The perfectly preserved Portland Castle – with walls 14 feet thick in places - was built by Henry VIII in 1540 as part of his coastal defences against invasion by the French.

Portland Stone is still being quarried today and is famous the world over after being used for buildings as diverse as St Paul's Cathedral, Broadcasting House and the United Nations Building in New York. Quarrying is believed to have begun in the Stone Age and the oldest stone construction on the island is the floor of the Culverwell Mesolithic site, circa 5200BC.

One word not to mention within earshot of a Portlander is 'rabbit'. The origins of the superstition that the word is unlucky remain unclear. It may have been beliefs transferred from the sacred hare in Celtic times or the damage rabbits were thought to do to quarries.

The giant breakwaters of Portland Harbour – the largest man-made structure in Dorset – were laid in Victorian times and provided four square miles of safe, deep water for the Navy. The wreck of the First World War battleship HMS Hood lies at the entrance to the southern access – scuttled in November 1914 to prevent attack by submarine.

busy waters
portland is home for many sports activities based around the harbour

IN
MEMORY
OF OVR
GLORIOVS
DEAD
1914 - 1918

memorial
the cenotaph at portland heights

■ natural monument: pulpit rock
at portland bill

the spirit of portland sculpture, above fortuneswell, depicts stone work and fishing, the two main industries of the isle

disused stoneworks near the lighthouse

bill's eye: coastwatch perched above the cliff

stone washed

gales throw waves into old stoneworkings near the bill

landmark
the portland bill lighthouse is 135 feet high and the light is visible for 26 miles

waterboard

portland is a busy commercial and recreational harbour

last light
from the beach at chiswell, portland

rock show
the red arrows play smoke on the water over portland and weymouth

COAST PATH

WESTON
2 MILES

CHURCH OPE COVE
2 1/2 MILES

light saver

the lighthouse on the bill, built in 1906, has helped many mariners find their way

chesil beach

eighteen miles of shingle bank,
graded by size, east to west

in association with

LLOYDS
property group

chesil beach

a unique and fascinating geological feature

THE Saxon word chesil, meaning shingle or pebble, gives its name to Chesil Beach, a shingle bank stretching 18 miles from Portland to West Bay.

This geographical wonder, part of Dorset's Heritage Coast, is thought to be unique, and as a result it has proved fascinating for geologists.

Created by Ice Age glacial movements around 80,000 years ago, it is a spit joined to the land at both ends. It has an even curve and a regular crest line, this being at sea level in the west, rising to 40ft high at Portland.

The pebbles, mainly flint and chert, are graded by size by an action of the sea called alutriation, with the largest at the Portland end and the size decreasing westwards down to shingle.

Stories of yesteryear say that sailors coming ashore on Chesil could tell where they were by the size of the pebbles.

One of the best views in Dorset is looking westwards from high on Portland. Here, on a clear day, one can see the magnificent curve of Chesil Beach and the adjoining Fleet stretching into the distance.

Protected behind Chesil Beach, stretching from Portland to Abbotsbury, the Fleet is a brackish lagoon and a Site of Special Scientific Interest. Some sediments in the Fleet are thought to be up to 7,000 years old.

For more than 600 years, a colony of hundreds of mute swans has made its home on the Fleet at Abbotsbury. Nowadays, from the end of May, visitors can wander safely around the nests at Abbotsbury Swannery and observe the fluffy cygnets at close quarters.

Chesil Beach is an excellent and well-known fishing beach, but is not, generally, a safe place for swimming, with the beach often steeply shelving with treacherous undertow currents.

did you know?

■ High above Abbotsbury on a 260ft hill is St Catherine's Chapel, a prominent landmark for seafarers. It was thought to have been built in around 1400 as a pilgrim chapel for Abbotsbury Abbey, which was destroyed during the Dissolution.

■ The church of St Nicholas in Abbotsbury still bears the visible scars of musket fire caused during a Civil War clash in 1664 when the Roundheads were besieged by Cavaliers in the church tower.

■ The small hamlet of Fleet was made famous by John Meade Faulkner's 1898 smuggling novel Moonfleet (and filmed by Fritz Lang in 1955 with Stewart Granger in the lead role), using the name of the prominent village family the Mohuns. Tales of secret underground passages persist to this day.

■ Although the village of Portesham is a little inland, the nearby 72ft Portland Stone Hardy's Monument at Blackdown is visible for miles around. It's nothing to do with famous Dorset author Thomas Hardy, but a tribute to Sir Thomas Masterman Hardy (1769-1839), the man to whom Lord Nelson is reported to have said: "Kiss me, Hardy".

■ Burton Bradstock, a pretty, compact village at the western end of Chesil Beach, is notable as being the home of entertainer Billy Bragg and for the National Trust-administered Hive Beach, where the Hive Beach Café has become renowned as much for the quality of its fish dishes as its superb position.

■ The Dam Busters' bouncing bombs, famously used in the raids on the Eder and Mohne dams in May 1943, were first tested by designer Barnes Wallis on the Fleet at the Chesil Beach Bombing Ranges in late 1942. A prototype bomb, pulled from the Fleet in 1992, can be seen at Abbotsbury Swannery.

royal guard
all swans remain property of the crown. here, on duty looking after the little ones

storm front

the shingle spit, seen from portland, weathers another fierce sea, protecting the fleet lagoon behind it

cold front

climbing temperatures call for a cool one on top of abbotsbury hill

harbour light

moored up in the fleet, and, right, light show at littlesea

graded grains

chesil beach curves away to the west. the stone size changes along its length, larger stones at the portland end, smaller towards west bay

coast

- ruins at abbotsbury
- south west coast path, marker stone at west bexington

stark
the silhouetted shape of portland, peeking at nearly 500ft high, sloping south towards the bill

angles
inviting waters on a hot day, but care must be taken with the steeply shelving beaches

high church

st catherine's chapel watching over chesil and the fleet lagoon, looking towards the sloping horizon of portland

west bay
to lyme regis

the oldest part of dorset's
world heritage coast

in association with

LLOYDS
property group

west bay to lyme regis

from tv's bridehaven to the landing point for royal rebellion

THE coastline between Burton Bradstock and Lyme Regis is one of rugged cliffs, huge beaches, landslides, fossils galore, sleepy villages and quirky towns.

It is also the oldest part of Dorset's Jurassic Coast, England's first natural World Heritage Site, with rocks dating from 200 million years ago.

The busy harbour village of West Bay (once known as Bridport Harbour) was an important port in Roman times and, as well as being a smallish working port today, it is also a popular holiday spot.

A remodelled harbour entrance has helped prevent disastrous flooding. Up the River Brit is Bridport, a place for 900 years associated with the rope-making industry, although also renowned as a brewing and market town.

A little to the west is Seatown, a village steeped in the history of smuggling, while nearby Chideock was mentioned in the Domesday Book, had a castle demolished in the Civil War and is now an area of outstanding natural beauty.

Golden Cap, near Seatown, is the highest cliff on the south coast of England at 619ft. Its name comes from the bare stretches of yellow earth (or weathered Upper Greensand), at its peak.

Charmouth is at the heart of the Jurassic Coast and the best place to find fossils.

Lyme Regis is a fascinating seaside town with a narrow tangle of streets tumbling steeply down to the harbour. A multi-million-pound sea defence and land stabilisation scheme in 2006 led to a brand new beach – with 71,000 tonnes of French sand and 41,000 tonnes of Isle of Wight shingle.

The 13th century sea wall, the Cobb, was made famous by Meryl Streep in the 1981 film The French Lieutenant's Woman.

did you know?

Pioneer geologist Mary Anning, the 'princess of palaeontology', whose fossil collecting led to the discovery of several species of long-extinct creatures, was born in 1799 where Lyme Regis' Philpot Museum now stands.

Charles II's illegitimate son, the ill-fated Duke of Monmouth, sailed from Holland to Lyme on June 11, 1685 and declared himself king in place of James II at the site of the Pilot Boat Inn. The rebellion was snuffed out and 12 Lyme men were hanged on the beach in the aftermath.

Lyme Regis's literary connections include Jane Austen staying in the town in 1804 and setting part of Persuasion in the town. John Fowles, author of the French Lieutenant's Woman, lived in Lyme until his death in 2005 and was town museum curator for a decade.

The short-lived BBC TV drama series Harbour Lights, starring Nick Berry, was filmed in West Bay, renamed Bridehaven. Hugh Fearnley-Whittingstall shot many elements of his River Cottage series in West Bay and Bridport.

The area around Charmouth is fantastic for fossiling, although prone to landslides. Black Ven, to the west of the village, has suffered most. Europe's largest coastal mudflow happened there in the winter of 1958/9, leaving countless fossils exposed. Many more landslips have followed.

The world's hottest chilli, the Dorset Naga, grown by Michael and Joy Michaud at their West Bexington market garden, has a scorching heat of around a million Scoville Heat Units, double the previous best. Anyone eating a whole one would require hospital treatment.

The Moores Family has been baking biscuits in Dorset since before 1860. The Morcombelake bakery was established in 1880, and the fifth generation continues making biscuits, including the famous Dorset Knob.

anchor point
lyme's nautical history dates back many centuries

brave face

walkers climbing east cliff at west bay as seagulls glide on the breeze rising over it

early riser
waves lap at west bay as the dawn lights east cliff

fenders out in west bay

lines out on the beach

haven
west bay harbour, the entrance has undergone major reconstruction

b i r d ' s   e y e
looking down on west bay harbour entrance and west along the coast towards lyme regis

coast

ENTER THIS SIDE
DEAD SLOW

B-774 · RNLI

■ doing the 'west bay wallow'
on boxing day

■ boats for hire on the river brit
at west bay

RIVER BOAT HIRE

life lyme

lyme regis lifeboat leaving west bay

golden cap from seatown. the name comes from the colour of the yellow earth that forms the peak of the headland. now it is largely covered in vegetation

Children Playing

Please clean up after your dog in the car park (including The grass)

In the Car Park (or on the Grass)

with stile
the coast path down to seatown beach

gold top
at 619ft golden cap is the highest peak on the south coast

time line
landslips make the charmouth seafront a rich area for geologists and fossil hunters, but care must be taken

CLOSED

DUE TO RECENT LANDSLIDES

down time
...for those who just want to relax or play there's always charmouth beach

storm fronts

these homes, on the prom at lyme, often feature in news coverage of severe gales

shore time

you can walk from charmouth to lyme along the front, but be sure of the tides

the cobb

the sea wall round the harbour at lyme regis, dating from the 13th century, famous for meryl streep's stormy scene in the french lieutenant's woman

green and gold
golden cap and lyme bay from the gardens, and the rocky shore

climbing flowers
...looking down over the beach and the cobb from lyme regis gardens

friendly invasion

lyme's beachfront has been replenished with sand from france and shingle from the isle of wight

r e f l e c t i o n s
wet sands pick up the colours on the front at lyme

resort to relaxation

taking time to enjoy the day

g u n   b o a t s
fishing boats aground, cannons silent on the harbour wall

cobb lit

three thousand candles on the cobb

who did what

design, graphics & captions:

john nesbitt

pictures:

sally adams, tony campbell, richard crease, john gurd,
jo harvell, graham hunt, brian jung, michelle luther,
corin messer, hattie miles, geoff moore, john nesbitt,
holly robinson, pat timmons, finnbarr webster

words:

maria court, nick churchill, cliff moore, robin thompkins

colour correction:

nick hayward

page make-up:

david hewitt, gary keeping, neil keeping,
john nesbitt, richard stone

commercial support:

shelley gorham

book sales:

steve court (01202 292250)

published by:

DAILY ECHO & **DorsetECHO**

in association with:

264 sandbanks road, lilliput, bh14 8ha
tel: (01202) 708044
36 haven road, canford cliffs, bh13 7lp
tel: (01202) 701800
www.lloydspropertygroup.com

air support

O ur grateful thanks go to Gary Ellson, and his team at Bournemouth Helicopters, whose skill and support made many of the pictures within these pages possible...

Bournemouth Helicopters, established in 1994, operate a modern fleet of Robinson R44 and Schweizer 300 helicopters.

They run courses for those who want to fly as a career, as transport or purely for pleasure, from private pilot's licence to mountain flying tuition.

Trial lessons are available for special occasions or business incentives, as are gift vouchers for all flights.
- Open 09:00 – 17:30, 7 days a week, 364 days a year
- Call 01202 590800
- www.bourne2fly.co.uk

picture this...

If you would like to order prints of one or more of the pictures in this book please...
- Call in to one of the Daily Echo offices and fill in an order form
- Visit bournemouthecho.co.uk and click on 'photographs'
- For further information call us on 01202 411307 or 411308
- Book sales: 01202 292250

Published by Newsquest Media (Southern) Ltd., Richmond Hill, Bournemouth, BH2 6HH.
First published in 2007.
Printed by Butler and Tanner, Frome, Somerset.
ISBN 0-9546280-5-5